Martin Zender
Goes To Hell

Also by Martin Zender

How to Quit Church
Without Quitting God

Martin Zender's Guide to
Intelligent Prayer

Flawed by Design

Martin Zender
Goes To Hell

Martin Zender

STARKE & HARTMANN

Martin Zender Goes To Hell

© 2004 by Martin Zender

Published by Starke & Hartmann
P.O. Box 6473
Canton, OH 44706
www.starkehartmann.com
1-866-866-BOOK

Printed in the United States of America

ISBN 0-9709849-1-X

To all who have lived
in unwarranted fear

"I was not commissioned except for the lost
sheep of the house of Israel."

—Jesus Christ
Matthew 15:24

"God is the Savior of all mankind,
especially of believers."

—Paul
1 Timothy 4:10

"It is the glory of God to conceal a matter,
but the glory of kings is to
search out a matter."

—King Solomon
Proverbs 25:2

INNER TURMOIL, PHASE I

Most of my life, I believed hell was an unimaginable place of frights, stalactites, and high temperatures, where the devil tormented people sent him by God. Why did the people get sent to hell by God? They were bad. They didn't meet God's standards. When I was eight years old, I really wanted to know what the standards were. I'm pretty sure I hated the idea of being tortured. I know I didn't want to go to The Bad Place. So I asked Father Passoli one gloomy Catholic day what the standards were. He said I had to go to Mass every Sunday. I said I thought I could handle that. I said it sounded easy. Was that all? Well, no.

"It would be even better if you stopped sinning," said the balding priest.

"Isn't that hard to do?" I asked.

"Yes," he said.

"Then I'll never make it."

"You must try," he said, and he bonked me on the head with his Bible.

"When is the last time *you* sinned," I boldly asked him, rubbing my head.

"1953."

The year was 1967.

"That's amazing," I said, and I fell into a kind of religious stupor until 1984.

TURMOIL, PHASE II

I quit the Catholic Church and became a Christian in 1979. My stupor continued for six more years, only now it was zealous. In July of 1984, I warned my mother about eternity in hell. I wasn't speaking generally, either. Well? My mother was still stuck in a religion of fear, not faith. She gave up chocolate during Lent, but a life devoid of candy does not salvation make. She had no living relationship with Christ that I could tell. In fact, like most Catholics, she equated the mere mention of His name—apart from chants and rotish prayers—with a form of freakery. (I bore the label "Jesus Freak" like an apostle of Christ. I suffered for His name's sake.) But here was the pressing point: Unless someone intercepted my mother's trajectory, she was headed for an eternity of conscious torment. I would do anything to prevent that. Who wouldn't?

I remember the day I phoned her. I remember where I was, how the phone felt in my hand, how the cord shook, the depth of my conviction. I tried to be nice, but how do you dangle hell before your mother in a civil and courteous fashion? I was doing her a favor. She would thank me for eternity. I was a good son. I was only thinking of her eternal well-being. I'm pretty sure these are all lies.

Why are you calling me about this? "Hell is an unimaginable place of frights, Mom, with stalactites and high temperatures. It's where the devil torments people sent him by God." *How does this apply to me?* "You're in love with your traditions. You don't meet God's standards." *And what are those standards?* "There's just one standard. Faith. You've got to do more than sit and stand and kneel, Mom. You've got to have faith." *Is that all?* "Well, no. It would be even better if you read the King James Bible every day." *Isn't that hard to do?* "Yes." *Then I'll never make it.* "You must try." *When is the last time you read it?* my mother boldly asked me. "This morning," said I. *That's amazing,* my mother said, and our relationship fell into a kind of stupor that has yet to wake all the way up.

MOTIVATION

I'd been reading The Good Book night and day since walking out of St. John's Catholic Church for the last time. The more I read and read my poor translation, the more I realized that I was responsible for saving my family. (Sorry, Jesus.) If I did not warn my mother about her dead religion and its consequence, then not only would she burn for eternity—even God knew that Catholics weren't saved—but I'd be held accountable for it. Who wants to meet God after botching something like that?

"Why didn't you tell her, Martin?"

"She was my mother. Can't we change the subject? Where's my wreath of righteousness?"

God would only shake His head. "You didn't love her."

"It was a touchy issue."

"Well, so is *this*..." and a sweep of His arm would reveal a scene worse than a nightmare: the woman who bore and nurtured me writhing in a sea of flame, unable even to look at me, or to beg, or to implore God for release. "And her punishments have only begun."

SLAM!

I would lose my hope and mind. Heaven would turn to hell, I would fall in tears at the Master's feet and…

Oh, creamy delivery—with peaches. No worries in heaven, friend! God thinks of everything. With a fell and lovely swoop, God would impart to me the much-anticipated mind of Christ. The Christian version of this wonderful gift is a mind that miraculously justifies the eternal torment of beings created in the image of God, for whom Christ died. It is a mind that justifies the never-ending agony of those once loved by the Deity. But wait. A special feature of the Christmind is the ability to consider the tormented as still loved. How can this be? In heaven, God's direst wrath is but a newer, higher manifestation of His love. As I said, all of this is miraculous. What new thoughts can the mind of Christ accomplish? Many. For this is an elaborate, divinely-altered mind to which the endless pain of a mother or father becomes "the glory of God." It is an amazing new mind to which the ceaseless cries of a son or daughter become comforting evidence of "the righteousness of God." Everything is more refined in heaven, you see. On this old, decrepit earth, the pains of our family cause *us* pain. Not so in Gloryland. There, love is perfected. Everything is new and improved. In heaven, we will look upon the agony of those we once nurtured with a kind of holy satisfaction. I wish I could describe it better for you. It will be quite lovely. Isn't it wonderful that we have this to look forward to?

A FLURRY OF TROUBLING QUESTIONS

Why are there so many translations of scripture, and why are they all different? Why can so many places in scripture be misinterpreted to teach the doctrine of eternal torment? Why is The Bible so confusing? Why did Jesus talk funny? Why does The Good Book cause so many fights and misunderstandings? Why does The Bread of Life break up families and make mothers call sons Jesus Freaks? Why is The Book With The Tasseled Bookmark so easily thumped and waved in the face? Why do people yell and scream while holding The Bible? What is it about The Black, Leather-Bound Word of God that makes people want to wear colorful robes and bonk children on the head?

RESOLUTION, PHASE I

Hello, and thank you for picking up this book. My name is Martin Zender. I'm a writer, a husband, a father, and a seeker. I assume that you're a seeker, too. Good. Jesus Christ began revealing His glories to me in June of 1985. I quit worrying in July. Only when I learned how to read the Bible critically did God unveil His depths. This may seem paradoxical, that glory should accompany diligent search and many broken pencils. I always thought it came when one's head was in the clouds, when one felt cozy and protected in church, when one floated through the day in a Big Warm Jesus Hug. No. These things, for me, led to self-righteousness, a rut of immaturity, and confronting my poor mother with the gospel of hell.

Then how does glory come? Absolutely, it comes from God. From our perspective, it comes from opening the eyes, from critically re-analyzing belief, from squarely facing previously ignored scripture. It comes from the determination to finally heed that still small voice that has whispered for years, *Something is missing.*

Might I suggest the missing thing to be a knowledge of the glory of God? Many people today who claim to love God are so busy attending church, singing, serving, praying, striving, talking, preaching, and vying for position, that they've forgotten what they're in this for. And that is to come to a realization of Who God is and what He is doing.

Do you really want to know? If not, then walk away now. Otherwise, prepare yourself to read the hardest sentence in the book.

RESOLUTION, PHASE II

*God purposely sends deceptions into the world—
even in the form of mistranslated scripture—to sepa-
rate truth lovers from the lovers of injustice.*

I'm glad you're here. I will quote you three scriptures to support this initially disturbing point.

Proverbs 25:2—"It is the glory of God to conceal a matter, and the glory of kings to investigate a
matter."

1 Corinthians 11:19—"For it must be that there
are sects also among you, that those also who are
qualified may be becoming apparent."

2 Thessalonians 2:11-12—"And therefore God
will be sending them an operation of deception, for
them to believe the falsehood, that all may be judged
who do not believe the truth, but delight in injustice."

We'll take these verses in reverse order, since the
last is the most troubling.

In the last days, God Himself will send an operation of deception. This is hard for many to take.
They say God would never do that, or anything like
it. But He would. He has done it before. In 1 Kings
22:23, God Himself put a deceiving spirit in the

mouth of King Ahab's prophets, to cause the king to fall at Ramoth Gilead. Read the verse for yourself: "Now therefore, behold, the Lord has put a deceiving spirit in the mouth of all these your prophets; and the Lord has proclaimed disaster against you." Now read Proverbs 25:2 again: It is the glory of God to *conceal* a matter, and the glory of kings to investigate.

God wants people to search, and He makes it so they have to. He hides truth—or situates it at an oblique angle—and then says, "Go find it. Show Me how badly you want it." If you want it, you'll spare no pains looking for it. You'll get down on your hands and knees if you have to. This happened to me, as I said, in 1985. But, as humans, we normally don't want to work that hard. We don't like pain. We have stiff joints and avoid bending over for anything. And so we'll generally just believe the popular "biblical" notion, especially if that notion suits our disposition and our pastor. There is a general disdain of investigation today among the religious, and church society has become the antithesis of the Bereans (Acts 17:11, the noble inhabitants of Berea) who searched the scriptures daily, refusing even to believe the likes of Paul.

Paul congratulated the Bereans for doubting him; he wanted them to search for themselves. Conversely, a lady where my wife works recently told her, "Stay away from me with that Greek stuff, Melody. God gave us pastors to teach us truth, and we have no right to question them. You turn over too many rocks." I'm glad I wasn't there. Melody is, too. Had I been there, I'd have said, "Really, Linda? And God gave us politicians, to teach us governing. Melody may turn over rocks, but you make Paul turn over in his grave."

God will be sending an operation of deception, *for them to believe the falsehood.* God Himself will send the deception. This is scripture talking, not me. God actually wants a large segment of the populace believing wrong things, and then defending their ignorance out of a misappropriated Bible. Why does

Melody raises hell wherever she goes.

God want this? So that those who believe the right things from That Book will become apparent. It's all about contrast. Read the three verses again; they must be faced. Stars do not visibly shine unless it's dark. Who made the dark? God did. Likewise, falsehood must exist in order for truth to be apparent, and God sends it. There is purpose in it; God knows what He's doing. Read the verse from 1 Corinthians again. There *must* be sects, even among the so-called believing populace.

Notice that the sects are among the Corinthians. This is not a problem outside Christianity. When I said there is a certain segment of the populace believing wrong things, I was not speaking of the world-at-large, but of those who call themselves followers of Christ. Are they truly followers of Christ, or have they merely fallen into convenient compartments that appear Christ-like? I'm just asking. The difference is subtle. Do you know people in compartments? It is so much easier to sink into a sect than to become a qualified worker who rightly divides the word of truth. There are fraudulent workers today, in the so-called Christian church. If you want to know who they are, don't look for the outwardly "evil" person. Don't bother with the leather jackets, the nose rings, the cigarettes. The fraudulent workers I speak of are Christian to the core, appearing to everyone—even to themselves—as apostles of Christ (see 2 Corinthians 11:13). If you want to identify them, get up close and sniff their doctrines.

Thanks again for sticking around. All of this is getting around to my subject of hell. Read the New Testament and notice that the doctrine of eternal torment appears, in some places, to be taught. But then so does the doctrine of Jesus saving the world, of the Lamb of God taking away the sin of the world, of death being abolished, of God reconciling all creation to Himself, of Satan's works being undone, and of good bettering evil. How can these opposing things appear to appear side-by-side in the same book? It's a mark, I believe, of divine genius. Please continue to the next paragraph.

God has so finely balanced His revelation that a person's disposition dictates what he or she sees there. If a person wants to see truth, it's there. (I intend to show you how there it is.) But if an individual delights in injustice, that is, if a person deep-down wants fellow-sinners to "get what's coming to them"—I call this injustice because God saves the saved by grace, yet somehow damns the damned for a lack of faith (*what happened to the grace?*)—then the person will find chapter and verse for that as well, though it be wholly misinterpreted.

Many Christians think they can't be deceived. That is the height of arrogance and an invitation to spiritual ruin. Everyone can be deceived. Peter was, Abraham was, Isaac was, Jacob was, yes, even after called by God. Deception hovers over my camp by the minute. And yours. When is a good time to let down our guard? Does the risk of deception cease after twenty-four years of following Christ? After forty? No. I'm never safe, and neither are you. Satan is the father of lies, and he's working overtime. If you think you can't be deceived, explain why God prescribes the armor of Ephesians, chapter six. I didn't mean to get testy. The armor protects us from the stratagems of the adversary.

Stratagems are lies.

Did you always believe? No. For a while, probably for years, God carried you in ignorance in anticipation of a better day. And what a stunning day that was. Why do you remember it? Because of the happy shock of darkness turning to light. Me, too. God did not do this *to* us, but for us. Every day we learn something new that we didn't know before, even in scripture. Prior to every revelation, we were ignorant. Possibly, we were deceived. After the awak-

A Christian man claiming he could never be deceived
once lived alone for thirty years in this windmill.

ening, we reveled in the new insight. Same book, new words. It feels good to learn, and God knows that. This is why He precedes the joy of revelation with the pain of ignorance. Because it feels so good when it stops? Yes. You must have your personal little sects, so that the brightness of revelation becomes apparent even among you—you, personally.

I pray that revelation shines upon you today.

Speaking of God's armor protecting us from Satan's lies, the biggest lie Satan has ever foisted upon the church and the world—under God's wise direction, of course—is the lie of eternal torment. (I have yet to prove this point, and I appreciate your patience. By the way, I am neither a Universalist, nor a Calvinist. Neither am I a somnambulist. No one has yet discovered an "ist" that fits me, except perhaps for "realist.") This is also the lie of the failure of God. If any are eternally tormented (or exterminated), then God's plan of saving them through Christ's sacrifice is thwarted. God wanted humanity saved, but most of humanity were too stubborn to accept His means, that is, the cross. Thus, the cross is not the all-powerful and universal thing we'd hoped it was, but an offer so weak that a single "no thanks" from a mortal human rebuffs it. This is a terrible lie because it makes God's will weaker than the human will, and evil greater than good. Worse, it makes the coming of Jesus the worst thing that ever happened to our race. Is this what you believe?

I meant what I just said. Think about it. Before the coming of Jesus, no one could go to hell. Why? Because no one can refuse a cross when there is no cross to refuse. After the cross, however, most the world is doomed because of the near-universality of rejecting it. The doomed will say, "Um, no thanks," and be damned. These three words, then, "Um, no thanks," and God's hands are tied, and down go the majority of mankind. But if no one refuses Jesus, then no one goes to hell. Agreed? But we all know how many people are going to hell. Millions. Millions, because Jesus came, the multitude saw, and the multitude turned away. Looking at this squarely, my conclusion is that the worst thing that ever happened to humanity, the very worst thing that could have happened to it, was the coming of Christ. Before Him, everyone was safe. After Him, the race is on probation, dangling by a thread over a cauldron of ceaseless torture. Is this what you believe? Do you ever even think about it? *Why* don't you think about it? Is it not important enough? Do you not need to know?

Where is the doctrine of eternal torment in the

Old Testament? If you don't know offhand, that's okay. I will taunt you with another question: What if it's not there? That's a big one. If this doctrine does not appear until New Testament times, it would mean that the most horrible doctrine ever to hit Earth was saved for the most loving (and only) Savior ever to leave Heaven.

I will now show you how the Old Testament contains not one word concerning the Christian doctrine of eternal torment.

WHERE IS THE GOD-AWFUL DOCTRINE?

When Adam sinned, what was the consequence? Go and see. Here was the worst sin ever. What better time to reveal the ultimate, horrible fate? But it's not there. You'll be driven from the Garden, Adam, and you'll have to hoe like mad to make anything grow. Eve, childbearing will introduce you to pain so severe you'll see white. And today, you begin to die, both of you. It's the penalty of your disobedience. Death and weeds and cramps the color of lightning. And I should mention this as well—I won't be coming around as often.

Bad enough, but not a word about an eternity of torture in flames. I wonder why. Do you?

Along comes Cain then, who murders his brother Abel. Murder is an unknown crime until then, but the worst since the Satan/Eve/fruit debacle. Now is a good time for God to unveil the Mother of All Punishments, to discourage future lawbreakers. But no, not a word about it. There is judgment, yes, but it's rational and reasonable: Cain's farming labors get cursed—the ground won't produce for him—and he has to wander the earth as a nomad. We anticipate such phrases as, "Burn forever, murderer," or, "Go to hell, Cain," but they are not here.

I hope no one is disappointed.

What about in the days of Noah? The citizens of that era sinned as a profession. All people thought about back then was: *How can we sin with more skill and greater efficiency?* They loved their grim occupation and rarely took a break from it. If any people deserved eternal torment, it was these. Burn the blasphemers in hell forever? Surprisingly, no. The sinners merely got wiped out in a flood. *Merely?* Think about it. One glug and down came your curtain. It couldn't have been pleasant, but it was better than burning forever.

God does sometimes employ fire and brimstone to curtail the careers of professional sinners. Like Lysol, however, fire and brimstone kill germs on contact. (That is, the fire and brimstone do not eternally torment the germs.) Consider the twin cities of Sodom and Gomorrah, cities which today have become synonymous with sexual perversion. When the hour of reckoning arrived, "The Lord rained on Sodom and Gomorrah brimstone and fire from the Lord out of heaven" (Genesis 19:24). The result? God "destroyed the cities of the valley" (verse 29). Note the conspicuous absence of "God began to torment the inhabitants of these cities for eternity."

Beats the heck out of eternal torment.

What about in the days of Moses, when there were laws for everything and a thousand ways to break them? Here's another ideal opportunity for the doctrine of eternal torment to begin "crawling all over scripture," as I've been told that it is. And yet, it is another opportunity squandered by God

and His servant Moses, who could get mad enough
to smash rock. All threats in the days of Moses concerned earthly rewards and punishments only. Kill
another man's bull, and your bull was killed. Mis-
handle some point of law, and your crops failed.
Tangle with Moses himself, and some terrible thing
happened with your wife's hormones. Or an enemy
would storm your gates. Or both.

All bad enough, but not crazy. Nothing eternal
and not a hint of unending flame. Capital punishment was by stoning then, the worst that could happen. It was nothing you wanted in on, but at least
you died. One rock to the head relaxed you enough
to dim the finish. No more taxes, tents, scorpions,
sand storms, or Moses. For men and women toiling
and failing upon an evil planet, death often came as
a mercy.

To review, nowhere in the Old Testament does
any God-inspired writer mention one word about
an eternity of torment for disobeying God. Not one
scholar has ever found it, no, not even those who
have searched for it desperately. Strange that a doctrine that is "everywhere" has not yet appeared in a
segment of the Bible that is, by my reckoning, about
three and a half inches thick.

Is it that the amateurs of that delicate era could
not shoulder such a responsibility? Then let the Old

Testament lightweights stand aside to make way for Someone Who Knows How To Damn. Close the Old Testament books, and make way for genuine terror. Turn one page past Malachi, all ye sinners. To the Gospels! But rejoice not. Rather, fear. For you did not realize how good you had it in the days of old. You are about to pine for those days of flood, famine, and stone. For here, finally, comes One Rising to New Levels of Damnation, a Divine Unveiler of Heretofore Unimaginable Torture. His Good News, in a nutshell, is "Love Me before you die, or my Father will do worse than kill you!" His name?

JESUS CHRIST, SAVIOR.

The spirit of the Lord is on Me, on account of which He anoints Me to bring the evangel to the poor. He has commissioned Me to heal the crushed heart, to herald to captives a pardon, and to the blind the receiving of sight; to dispatch the oppressed with a pardon, to herald an acceptable year of the Lord...

—*Jesus Christ*, Luke 4:18-19

Are you ready now to find out how things *really* are?

What follows is the meat of this treatise, a look
at places in scripture that appear to teach eternal
torment, but don't. In most cases, my job will be
simply to shine a small beam of light into an unno-
ticed cranny of the passages. This is to cause you to
see something that has always been there but that
you never saw. Of course, you may not want to see
what appears. I have no idea what condition your
heart is in. If your heart is pliable, you will want to
see, and you will. It is hard for me to imagine a heart
unwilling to appreciate a more glorious God, but
there are plenty such hearts; I've met some. Heaven
just won't be the same for them if so-and-so makes
it.

For the rest of you, here we go. Remember, God
did this on purpose. Do not resent the years you
spent not knowing this. This was God's plan, to thrill
you with the light of revelation you receive today.

**When Jesus Christ was on earth, neither He
nor His disciples heralded a worldwide gospel.**

Matthew 10:5-7, "These twelve Jesus commis-
sions, charging them, saying, 'Into a road of the
nations you may not pass forth, and into a city of
the Samaritans you may not be entering. Yet be going rather to the lost sheep of the house of Israel.

Now going, herald, saying that "Near is the kingdom of the heavens!"""

If this is mankind's one and only chance to "believe in Jesus or go to hell for eternity," then Jesus has a funny way of getting out the news. "Don't tell this to ninety-nine percent of the human race," He basically says. "Keep with Israelites."

I have yet to meet an orthodox preacher who can explain this. In fact, it causes much stammering among them. It is a round hole into which their square doctrines do not fit. They already know "for sure" that Jesus is laying out the conditions for all mankind to be either saved or damned for eternity, and so they haven't the objectivity to hear what He's actually saying.

First of all, what is the kingdom of the heavens spoken of here? Is it heaven itself? No. It is the kingdom *of* the heavens; that is, it is heavenly in character, but it is located on the earth. It's a period of a thousand years of relative peace on this oblate spheroid, when Jesus Christ, along with a reborn Israel, will rule the nations. It will be the reward of saintly Israelites then to "live and reign with Christ a thousand years" (Revelation 20:4), "on the earth" (Revelation 5:10). This is also known as the Millennium. It's no piece of fiction, or figure of speech, but a well-predicted event coming to an era near you.

If you don't believe me concerning Jesus' message, then believe Jesus Himself: "I was not commissioned except for the lost sheep of the house of Israel (Matthew 15:24)." How did we miss these simple words? This is what I meant about God hiding things. The words are there, but we somehow don't see them. Paul confirms Christ's confession, writing in Romans 15:8, "For I am saying that Christ has become the Servant of the Circumcision, for the sake of the truth of God, to confirm the patriarchal promises." That's three witnesses for you. The patriarchal promises were those promises God made to Abraham centuries before, that his seed would eventually rule earth. For how long? Once it started, the kingdom would last a thousand years.

Appreciate what this means. It means that all of Jesus' words (the words printed in dark red in your New Testament) concern one people: Israel. And all the threats He directed toward those people—the fire, the worm, the curse of the goats, the separation of the bad fish, the uprooting of the tares, the burning of the branches—concerned entrance or refused entrance into the coming millennial kingdom—*only.* The issue was neither heaven nor hell. It was not, as I have read on so many church signs, "Where will you spend eternity?" The *topic du jour* was this and this only: "Will you or will you not enter into the thousand-year kingdom and be blessed there?"

What would happen after the thousand years? That's a good question, one that Jesus never broached while on earth. He did address it, later, through an apostle of His choosing: Paul. But here is another question, related to the first: What of those poor Israelites disbarred from the kingdom? Are they banished forever from the presence of God? The answer to that question will change your life. Jesus did give a definite answer, but again, not a word of it while on earth. The answer is not printed in red. He gave the answer later from His exalted throne through the writings of the previously mentioned apostle. I'll quote from some of his writings later. But first, I want to elaborate upon Jesus' red-lettered threats.

Better to lose an eye or a hand than to burn.

The most frightening threats Jesus made to the Israelites are probably those found in Matthew 5:29-30 and Mark 9:43-48. Here, Jesus explains how much better it is for an Israelite to pluck out his or her eye, or tear off his or her hand, than to let these members lead one into "the fire of hell." These verses have terrified countless millions over the centuries, people to whom the verses don't even apply. So much senseless worry over eyes and limbs. These are Israelite threats for an Israelite kingdom.

The fire of hell? That's bad translating. Jesus never said the word "hell" in His life. Well? He didn't speak English. The word that left His lips was *Geenna.* That's right. Jesus warned the Israelites about "the fire of Gehenna," not hell, and any concordance will confirm this for you (see word #1067 in Strong's, and page 474 in Young's.) Gehenna is a small valley along the southwest corner of Jerusalem. It's a geographical location, a place you can walk in today. It's a pleasant little valley now. You can fly to Jerusalem and walk in hell. Have a picnic there with your family. Have a hell of a time. Get yourself an Auto Club map and go to hell. God made sure that some versions of scripture got this right (the Concordant

Off to hell with family.

Copyright by C.S. Hammond & Co., N.Y.

Literal New Testament, Rotherham's Emphasized Bible, and Young's Literal Translation, to name three); others He perfectly warped, so that those who are qualified may be becoming apparent.

As any dictionary will tell you, Gehenna is where the Israelites of old dumped their garbage and offered sacrifices to foreign gods. In the old days it was called the Valley of Hinnom. From the Random House Dictionary, under the entry *Gehenna*: "the valley of Hinnom, near Jerusalem, where propitiatory sacrifices were made to Molech." It may be a pleasant green valley today, but in the thousand-year kingdom it will function as a crematorium for the corpses of criminals. Don't be shocked. Unlike today, judgment during the kingdom era will be swift and sure, and criminals will think twice before breaking the law.

The fire of hell? Here is the only instance where the King James Version has taken the name of an actual place and made it something else. Watch this: Where the Greek has *Hierousalem*, the KJV translates "Jerusalem"—every time. Where the Greek has *Nazaret,* the KJV makes it "Nazareth"—every time. Where the Greek has *Bethleem*, the KJV has "Bethlehem"—every time. This is sensible. It's an honorable and consistent way of translating. But here, where Jesus says *Geenna* (another geographical location), the KJV (as well as the New International Version—NIV—and New American Standard Bible—NASB), makes it "hell." Gee, that's weird. Can you explain it? I can. Ever hear the phrase, "theological bias?"

The Israelites trembled to hear the name Gehenna. They knew what Jesus was talking about. It had nothing to do, in their minds, with eternal torment. Their prophet Isaiah had written about the place centuries before:

All flesh shall come to worship before Me in Jerusalem, says Yahweh. And they fare forth and see the corpses of the mortals, the transgressors against Me, for their worm shall not die, and their fire shall not be quenched, and they become a repulsion to all flesh.
—Isaiah 66:23-24

See anything Fishy?

No sane person would swallow the idea of a billion people suffering forever in a **2500 X 200 ft. valley** southwest of Jerusalem. So, to maintain the false fear of eternal torment, the **KJV, NIV & NASB translators** suddenly turned a geographical location into a mythological torture chamber.

Geographical location, in original	As translated in KJV, NIV, NASB
Hierousalem	Jerusalem
Kapharnaoum	Capernaum
Nazaret	Nazareth
Bethania	Bethany
Ephesion	Ephesus
Bethleem	Bethlehem
Bethsaida	Bethsaida
Kappodokia	Cappadocia
Beroia	Berea
Gomorra	Gomorrah
Galilaia	Galilee
Damaskos	Damascus
Geenna	hell *(-say what??)*

Matthew 5:29, 30; 10:28; 18:9; 23:15, 33

With the worms and the fire, this is obviously the Gehenna Jesus referred to. The key word in the prophecy is "corpses." This is the word you haven't noticed before, and it's where I shine my light. Here is the word that clarifies the topic. There are a few smoldering corpses in Gehenna, not ten billion writhing zombies. No one has ever seen a writhing corpse, I trust. Gehenna is as practical as can be. The fire and the worms consume the old corpses, making room for new ones. It's gruesome, yes, but not the phantasmagoric scene the Christian religion has made it.

Writhing Corpses?

Note that the Hebrew does not say that the worms would *never* die, or that the fire would *never* go out. As long as there are corpses to feed them, the worms "shall not die," and the fire "shall not be quenched." (When an emergency room doctor tells a distraught mother, "Your son shall not die," he does not mean *ever*.) Neither does the Greek speak of eternal worms and flames. Rather, it calls the fire "unextinguished" and the worm "not deceasing." Just as a house fire is "unextinguished" until someone puts it out, and a healthy man is "not deceasing" until he contracts a disease and dies, the fire and the worm will serve God's purpose undisturbed until He finishes with them. And finish with them He will. This is by no means God's ultimate goal.

Jesus' threat adjusted many a slack Israelite. No sane son of Jacob longed for corpsehood, especially not during the kingdom era. The goal was to rule and reign with Christ, not smolder among the dead.

How could such a distortion occur, and how could so many people fall for it? Surprisingly, it's not that hard to make a small valley outside Jerusalem equipped to handle but a few dozen corpses during a thousand-year kingdom, into a place where God will consciously burn billions of sinners forever. It's not hard, that is, if this is what a person wants the place to be. All it takes is a little bit of squinting, a cocking of the head at a forty-five degree angle, and a thick pair of tinted glasses.

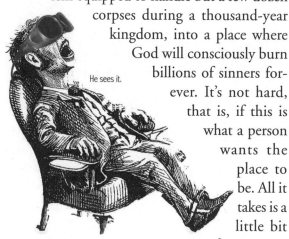

He sees it.

It is tempting to blame such skewed vision on prejudice, carelessness, pride, a vengeful heart, bad study habits, or—in the case of pastors—a desire to scare people into church. And relatively speaking, this would be right. But looking at this from an absolute viewpoint, we may be wiser to credit God. God could have easily given the translators of our bestselling versions the wisdom to keep *Gehenna* the way His Son said it. He could have easily brought forward Isaiah's "corpses" into the New Testament contexts. Wouldn't these simple moves have saved the world a churchload of deception? Yes. But God refused to do either of these things. Why? Didn't He know what would happen? Of course He knew; He's God. *God did it on purpose.* Behold, the genius of God. God purposely warped our bestselling versions to force us to seek. He purposely hid the right answer, to give kings the honor of searching it out. If we want to seek truth, it's there; God does not shut a door on one portion of scripture without opening a window elsewhere. No one can ever accuse Him of making it impossible. But if a person would just as well see stupid, disobedient sinners get punished for eternity, then the snare of "hell" is lying at the door.

Walk right in.

"And these shall go away into everlasting punishment: but the righteous into life eternal."

This is the King James version of Matthew 25:46. Here we find "the Son of Mankind come into His glory, seated on the throne." In front of Him are gathered "all the nations," and "He shall be severing them from one another even as a shepherd is severing the sheep from the goats." He shall be "standing the sheep at His right, yet the goats at the left." You know the rest. The sheep go to heaven; the goats go to hell—forever. Bleat, baaaa, and bye-bye. The judgment accomplished, Jesus stands up, washes His hands in the manner of Pilate, then departs with a crisp, "That's that."

This judgment is advertised in your local church as "the final judgment" of "all mankind," when "God's enemies" go to either "heaven or hell," for "all eternity." But as you may have guessed by now, it's nothing of the kind. This ingenious snare has exposed the unwitting injustice of the Christian religion.

The first place to shed light is upon the word "nations." It's the key at the door. But God so quickly employs the sheep/goat analogy that the casual reader drops the key. *Must be individuals*, the reader thinks. *He's standing them at His right and left*. But no. Each sheep and goat represents a nation, not a person. This is not Uncle Harry standing before Jesus; it is Ethiopia. This is not Aunt Hazel trembling before Him; it is Russia. It is not Jim the milkman; it is Afghanistan.

This judgment occurs at the inauguration of the thousand-year kingdom, in the valley of Jehoshaphat. Like Gehenna, this is a literal, geographical location outside Jerusalem (see map again on page 37). In fact, it's right around the corner from Gehenna. It's known today as the Kidron Valley. Fly there and sniff the daffodils. The judgment here will be the fulfillment of the prophecy of Joel 3:1-2:

> For, behold, in those days, and in that season, when I shall turn back the captivity of Judah and Jerusalem, I will also convene all the nations and bring them down to the valley of Jehoshaphat. And I enter into judgment with them there concerning My people, and My allotment, Israel, Whom they disperse among the nations.

As with Gehenna's fire and worms, this judgment is practical. Jesus returns to find earth's political alignments amok. Good nations will be low; the evil will sit on high. The Great Judge will cure this.

He will gather all the nations before Him (the nations' representatives, likely), in this valley, to determine their situation. What criteria will He use for judging? Their belief in Him? Their confession of faith? The mode of their baptism? No. It will be that nation's policy toward Israel, nothing more. Nothing of faith here, or of belief. Read the context and see for yourself. No one will ask, "What church did you go to?" or, "Why didn't you have more faith?" If the nation helped Israel in her hour of trial ("Whatsoever you do to these, the least of My brethren, you do to Me"), that nation will be placed near the capital city, Jerusalem. If not, then off to one of the four corners of earth. Near nations will be blessed, far nations not so much. Here, at the far corners, we find the "outer darkness" and the "gnashing of teeth." A dentist will do brisk business.

Whereas the Gehenna deception requires a forty-five degree head cock, here the neck must be craned to the bottom of the compass. To make this practical scene in a Middle-East valley the final damning of all unbelievers, for all time, nations must be turned to individuals. This is but the first distortion. Next, the scriptural criteria of judging, that is, "How did you treat Israel?" must be changed to, "Did you have faith in Jesus Christ as your personal Savior?" Then, lovers of injustice face the unenviable task of raising billions of people from the dead before their time. What do I mean? Most of mankind will not even be alive during this judgment, which takes place at the beginning of the thousand years. Note: "The rest of the dead do not live until the thousand years should be finished" (Revelation 20:5).

But who cares? I realize that no matter what facts I bring to light, many people will still believe what they want to believe. Most Christians don't really care what actually happens in this valley, as long as they, themselves, are saved. Truth be known, the possibility of a near-universal twisting of this judgment, of a vast misrepresentation of God's character, of billions of people their pastors told them would be judged here being stone dead at the time, will not bother them. Why? Because to be bothered will eventually mean to admit to consequential error, a thing too hard for most people to do.

Why should such a confession be hard? Isn't revelation the Great Christian Jewel? No. The Great Christian Jewel is Acceptance By Other Christians. The Great Christian Jewel is Community. The Great Christian Jewel is: I Could Never Be Deceived. I realize that Christians "adore Christ." I know they "love God." But I am speaking here of the Great Christian Jewel.

What price revelation? It's not that exorbitant,

really. It's only this, to say, "I was wrong. I misread this judgment. And because of this, I misjudged God's character, a more serious mistake. I believed what I was taught. I admit now that I had not considered it critically, for myself." This is not humiliation. It is liberation. But return with me now to reality. In the church today, any truth that endangers community will be shunned. No one to whom fellowship is the vital thing will even consider a truth that may rock the boat. *God's character is at stake? Oh, well.* There is too real a fear, in organized religion, of the sideways glance. But I am not writing

"Shut up with your stupid facts! Everyone is looking at me!"

to those who fear man. I am writing to those to whom the following question matters: "What is God actually doing in this valley, and how does it reflect upon His Son dying for mankind?" I am writing to those willing to concede a former blindness in light of a new-shining truth.

The proper translation of Matthew 25:46 is, "And these shall be coming away into chastening eonian, yet the just into life eonian." This is right. The Greek word mistranslated eternal (see word #166 in Strong's, and page 311 in Young's) is *aionion.* The perfect English equivalent is "eonian." This is the adjectival form of "eon," a word the dictionary defines as a period of time. God is speaking of time here, not eternity. To translate this word "everlasting" or "eternal" is to alter its meaning. No, worse. It's to give it a meaning opposite of what it means. One may as well translate the Greek word meaning light, "dark," or the Greek word meaning up, "down." Eternity is the opposite of time.

Have I told you yet what a concordance is? Looking back, I see that I haven't. A concordance is a large reference volume that lists every word used in scripture, along with the Hebrew or Greek word behind it. It weighs about five pounds, and it really hurts if you drop it on your foot. It costs about the same as a pair of blue jeans. As I have already suggested, God would not make a Phillips screw head without providing the proper driver. But you need to buy the screwdriver. You need to go to your local bookseller and buy the proper tool.

This is my *Young's Analytical Concordance*, page 313. Youngs has "ages of the ages" for *tous aionas ton aionon*, which is pretty good.

Anyway, the mistranslation of this word has gotten versions like the King James into trouble. As a notable and embarrassing example, compare Revelation 11:15 with 1 Corinthians 15:25. From the King James Version:

Revelation 11:15, "The kingdoms of this world are become the kingdoms of our Lord and of His Christ; and He shall reign for ever and ever."

1 Corinthians 15:25, "For He must reign till He hath put all enemies under His feet."

Does scripture contradict itself? Scripture doesn't, but the King James Version (as well as the NIV and the NASB) does, and you're looking at it. Does Jesus reign forever and ever, or does He reign only until He has put all enemies under His feet?

Both cannot be true. Answer: He reigns only until He has put all enemies under His feet.

"Forever and ever" is a mistranslation of the Greek phrase *tous aionas ton aionon*, which is properly translated "for the eons of the eons." Eons are long periods of time during which God gradually reconciles all creation to Himself. After these eons, when God has reached His goal, Christ gives up His reign—and Himself—to God. This isn't me talking, it's 1 Corinthians 15:28. Jesus reigns so well during the eons that reign becomes unnecessary at their conclusion. Follow me here. A king who reigns requires subordinates. Right? But this is an imperfect state. God's goal is to bring everyone into perfect oneness with Himself (see 1 Corinthians 15:28 again; the inspired phrase is "all in all"). Who accomplishes this perfection on God's behalf? Christ does. Rejoice and be glad. No one insisting, "Jesus reigns forever!" is doing Him a favor. In fact, Christ would count it as an insult. Were you to insist upon this to a knowledgeable believer, that believer would remark facetiously, "He reigns forever? Drats. I was rather hoping God would become all in all."

When properly translated, both these verses are true. When mistranslated in the manner of the common versions, one of them has to be false.

The solution? A correction of the single mistranslated word. The result? A Bible that doesn't contradict itself. And the "everlasting punishment" and "life eternal" of Matthew 25:46 become merely the "chastening eonian," and "life eonian" experiences of bad and good nations during the Millennium. The bad nations will be chastened then (the "fire" of verse 41 refers figuratively to that), the good nations will generally enjoy themselves. Beyond that, nothing is said of mankind's eternal fate. To make this verse speak of mankind's eternal fate is to burden it beyond its purpose. *So far, at this point in revelation, we have no statement concerning mankind's eternal fate; sin is still undied for.*

Appreciate the genius of God; one little penny on the track (the mistranslated word) sends the whole train flying. But remember, "It is the glory of God to conceal a matter, and the glory of kings to investigate a matter" (Proverbs 25:2). An hour's investigation, and you will see it. Swallow it blindly, and you'll crash with the train.

"Verily, verily, I say unto thee, Except a man be born again, he cannot see the kingdom of God…Marvel not that I said unto thee, 'Ye must be born again.'"

This is John 3:3, 7 from the King James Version. I saw this verse splayed recently in two-foot tall letters upon a billboard in a large city. It was put there by a mega-Baptist church trying to save the city from hell. What the Baptists wanted this sign to say was: "If you idiotic residents of this large city do not figure out how to get reborn, and soon, you'll be separated from God forever." But is this what Jesus was saying to Nicodemus on a quiet Tuesday night outside the temple? Not at all.

Stay with the program. Remember the program? Jesus is preaching the thousand-year kingdom to Israelites only. He was not commissioned except to the lost sheep of the house of Israel. Nothing has changed. This message was specifically designed for Nicodemus and his fellow Israelites, not for the rush hour rat racers of twenty-first century Buffalo.

Note the "ye" of verse seven. This is the word you haven't seen before. "Ye" is the Old English plural of "you." Jesus is saying to Nicodemus, "*You people* must be born again." An individual man can be born again only as part of a reborn nation. First and foremost, this was a call for the rebirth of Israel. Nicodemus thinks Jesus is talking about a literal womb, and he proceeds to ask a ridiculous question. Jesus chides him in verse 10: "You are a teacher of Israel, and these things you do not know?"

Nicodemus should have known because the famous prophet Isaiah wrote of it way back in Isaiah 66:8-9—

"Who has heard such a thing? Who has seen such things? Can a land be born in one day? Can a nation be brought forth all at once? As soon as Zion travailed, she also brought forth her sons. Shall I bring to the point of birth, and not give delivery?" says the Lord? "Or shall I who gives delivery shut the womb?" says your God.

And so the famous "born again" passage—the darling of Christendom—has nothing to do with the eternal fate of mankind-at-large. It has to do with the nation Israel getting a new heart for the Millennium. If an Israelite refuses his part in the born-again nation, that Israelite will not see the kingdom of God. And what, again, is the kingdom of God? It's the same that it has been up to this point. An eternity in heaven? No; a thousand years on earth.

"For God so loved the world, that He gave His only begotten Son, that whosoever believeth in Him should not perish, but have everlasting life" (John 3:16).

Jesus is still talking to Nicodemus. The Greek

word mistranslated "everlasting" is *aionion* again. To repeat, eonian is the adjectival form of the noun "eon," which is a period of time. As goes a noun, so goes its adjective (i.e. day/daily, hour/hourly). If an eon is a period of time, which it is, then eonian must have a time tint also, which it does. This verse is rightly translated, "For thus God loves the world, so that He gives His only-begotten Son, that everyone who is believing in Him should not be perishing, but may be having life eonian."

In the context of John 3:16, "life eonian" pertains only to life during the thousand-year kingdom. Thus, the "perishing" deals also with the same period. Of what? *Of time.* Whoever is believing in Him will enjoy the thousand-year life. Conversely, whoever does not believe will be perishing then. This is all Jesus is attempting to say to Nicodemus. What happens after that? At this point we don't know. John 3:16 doesn't know, and neither does it care. It's not paid to care. John 3:16 cares only for the thousand-year kingdom and who's going to be there. God proves to the world His love by sending His Son to rescue Israelites who will eventually rule the world in righteousness. To push John 3:16 past its design in this context is to murder it. It's to throw a fish from an airplane and tell it to fly.

The difference, then, between what Jesus

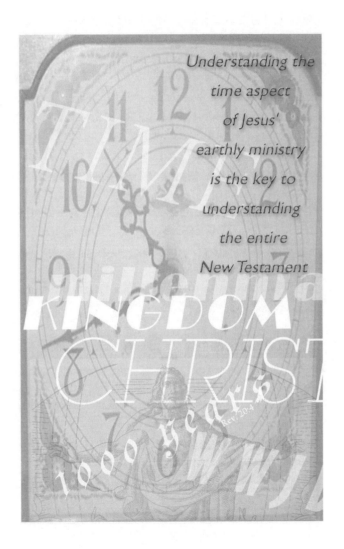

Understanding the time aspect of Jesus' earthly ministry is the key to understanding the entire New Testament

preached and what He's presumed to have preached is this one little thing, which is big as can be: THE TIME FACTOR. It's not just here in John 3:16, but in all other "everlasting" contexts. Correct the one word, and Jesus' earthly ministry shines truer. Correct the one word, and God's ultimate goal for redeeming creation bursts forth from other corners of scripture. Lay the penny of eternity on the rail, however, and away goes Jesus' ministry *and* God's goal, over the cliff.

Nothing here implies that unbelievers will stay that way, or that perishing people will never see life. After all, look what God is doing with you and me.

"Narrow is the way that leads to life, and few there be who find it" (Matthew 7:14).

True enough—concerning the thousand-year kingdom.

"And everyone who shall be declaring a word against the Son of Mankind, it shall be pardoned him, yet the one who blasphemes against the holy spirit shall not be pardoned" (Luke 12:10).

What about "the unforgivable sin?" *Did* Jesus say there is a sin that will never, ever go away? Obviously He didn't, or He would deny His own mission, described by a celestial messenger in Matthew 1:21 as: "He shall save His people from their sins." If but one of His people retains but one of his or her sins, He will have botched His mission. What our Lord did say was that there was a sin that wouldn't be forgiven. There's a big difference between that and a sin that will never, ever go away. This is much simpler than it sounds, and I'll explain what I just said in a moment. But first, here are the two other passages that fuel the argument. From the Concordant Literal New Testament:

Mark 3:28-29- "Verily, I am saying to you that all shall be pardoned the sons of mankind, the penalties of the sins and the blasphemies, whatsoever they should be blaspheming, yet whoever should be blaspheming against the holy spirit is having no pardon for the eon, but is liable to the eonian penalty for the sin."

Matthew 12:32- "And whosoever may be saying a word against the Son of Mankind, it will be pardoned him, yet whoever may be saying aught against the holy spirit, it shall not be pardoned him, neither in this eon nor in that which is impending."

It is clear that the persons committing the sin of blaspheming the holy spirit will not be released from whatever penalty God has fit for it. The obvious question now should be: What is the penalty for this sin? People assume that it's eternal separation from God in a flaming pit of torture. Hmm. Am I not reading closely enough between the lines? Where does either text say that? Nowhere. Yet such an unscriptural penalty is read into these passages. I refuse to say less about these passages than what the Lord has said; I won't deny His words. But neither will I add to them.

Mark 3:28-29 contains a clue: The penalty for this sin is eonian, not eternal. That means it is limited to time. Let's look further, noting the progression of detail in Matthew 12:32.

This sin will not be pardoned, "neither in this eon nor in that which is impending." Which eon is impending? The thousand-year kingdom of Israel's earthly reign, the very kingdom He came proclaiming. Those committing this sin, then, will miss that kingdom. It's that simple. In rejecting the spirit, they forfeit eonian life. A stiff penalty? Yes, but not a stupid one. One sin sown does not eternal torment reap. Otherwise, the Savior who died to save His people from their sins didn't quite do it.

Let's say a man robs a grocery store and serves a two-year jail sentence. Is he forgiven? No. His sin is not pardoned. We might say, "the man who robs a grocery store will not be pardoned." And he's not.

He goes to jail, does his time, then is released. A week later, we see him eating lunch at Wendy's. Are we shocked? Appalled at a travesty of justice? No. This man paid his debt to society, and now he's free.

Get the point? It does not follow that because this man was not pardoned, he is never released from prison. Neither does it follow that because an Israelite is not forgiven his blasphemy of the holy spirit, he will never be saved. Remember, God is the Savior of all mankind (1 Timothy 4:10), and Jesus came to save His people from their sins (Matthew 1:21).

"Bugsy here wants to know why he got eternity for double parking."

Besides, this threat of no forgiveness for two eons for this particular sin applies only to those Israelites who ignored the counsels of Jesus, and only for the time specified. This has nothing to do with the body of Christ, so stop wringing your hands over someone else's bill. (How many have imagined that they've committed this sin and blown their salvation? Blame the clergy for the ensuing mental trauma.) Neither has it anything to do with the time subsequent to the coming eon.

Every Israelite knew about the coming eon. That would be the eon when they, with Messiah, would rule the earth for a thousand years. They all wanted in on that. But most didn't know that Jesus Christ was the Way.

What Jesus was saying to these Israelites was: "Look. You people can trash me all you want. But if you trash the spirit that empowers me, you're in a bad way. There is no forgiveness for that sin either now, in this eon, or in the coming eon, which you know well to be the thousand years of peace."

Those words would have twisted an Israelite's gut. Israelites ate, breathed, and slept that eon, to "reign with Him a thousand years" (Revelation 20:6).

I could wish some soul had raised his hand at this point and asked: "Okay, Jesus. No forgiveness for that sin now or then. Got that. No kingdom glory for spirit blasphemers. Serves them right. It's the eonian penalty for them; they'll miss all the hoopla of that great eon. I've got no problem with that, Teacher. You won't find *me* blaspheming the spirit. But Teacher. What happens *after* the kingdom? What happens to these people and their sin *after* that eon?"

That would have been a great question. Likely Jesus would have answered in accord with Matthew 1:21-

"I'll be saving them from their sins, of course."

"And thou, Capernaum, which are exalted unto heaven, shalt be brought down to hell: for if the mighty works, which have been done in thee, had been done in Sodom, it would have remained until this day" (Matthew 11:23, KJV).

Can a whole city fit into the valley of Gehenna? Not without some radical bulldozing. But this time, Jesus didn't say *Geenna*, He said, *hades*. I know this because I looked it up in my concordance. Don't be upset that there's another word mistranslated "hell." It's not my fault. I'm not going to be gradually hitting you with a dozen more words. These are the only two words, spoken by Jesus, that have been mistranslated "hell." Thanks to the KJV, the NASB and the NIV, the only way to tell these apart is with a reference tool. Hades is no more a place of eternal torment than Gehenna. All the word means is "unseen." The first part of the word, [h]a means "un," (a is the Greek negative—and ours as well, as in "asymmetrical"), and ades is "perceived." Hades is any aspect of the universe that evades our five senses.

In Acts 2:31, the King James Version has Peter saying of Christ, "His soul was not left in hell, neither His flesh did see corruption." This should prove once and for all the unworkability of the standard translations. Did Jesus go to the Christian place of eternal torment? Um, no. And neither did He preach there. (You're probably thinking of Peter's later statement in 1 Peter 3:19, that Jesus preached to spirits in jail. This could not have occurred while Jesus was dead, obviously. It occurred after He had been "vivified in spirit" [verse 18], that is, after His resurrection. And He did not visit tormented humans in the flaming pit of Christian torture. Rather, He "heralded to spirits in jail…to those once stubborn, when the patience of God awaited in the days of Noah." These are spiritual beings, not humans. Humans, in scripture, are never called spirits. These are the supernatural beings [evil spirits] that had compelled the race toward destruction in the days of Noah. As far as I can tell, they are immortal. They are the subterranean dwellers mentioned in Philippians 2:10, one of three classes of beings that shall bow the knee and acclaim the Lordship of Jesus Christ. Peter actually identifies the place of their incarceration as "the gloomy caverns of Tartarus" [2 Peter 2:4]. Here, incidentally, is the third and final word that our illustrious/shiftless translators have made "hell," the only "hell" not mentioned by Jesus. Three words in all, then, *hades, Geenna,* and *Tartarus,* all lazily lumped into the inglorious catch-all "hell." Do you feel deceived? Well, it's over now. God is lifting the veil.)

What did Peter actually say concerning Christ? "He was neither forsaken in the unseen, nor was His flesh acquainted with decay." In other words, not only did God rescue Christ from the realm of imperception, He spared His body the ignominy of decomposition. God roused Christ.

HELL, THE REAL DEFINITION

Our English word hell is derived from the Anglo-Saxon *helan,* which means, "to cover, conceal, or hide." This is the precise meaning of the Greek *hades,*

4. 7 the sons of H. (were) Zereth, and Jezoar

HE'-LAM, חֵלָם הֵלָם.
A place E. of the Jordan, but W. of the Euphrates. Perhaps it is identical with *Alamatha*, on the W. of the Euphrates, near Nicephorium.
2 Sa. 10. 16 they came to H.; and Shobach..(went) be.
10. 17 and passed over Jordan, and came to H.

HEL'-BAH, חֶלְבָּה *fertility*.
A town in the tribe of Asher, near Achzib.
Judg. 1. 31 did Asher drive out the inhabitants of..H.

HEL'-BON, חֶלְבּוֹן *fruitful*.
A city celebrated in ancient times for the quality of its wine. It still bears its ancient name *Helbon* and is a village within a few miles of Damascus and still celebrated for producing the finest grapes in the country. The Arabic name *Halbûn* contains the Hebrew equivalents exactly.
Eze. 27. 18 thy merchant..in the wine of H., and white w.

HELD —
To be hidden, חָבָא *chaba*, 2.
Job 29. 10 nobles held their peace, and their tongue

HELD in, to be —
To curb, בָּלַם *balam*.
Psa. 32. 9 whose mouth must be held in with bit and

HEL'-DAI, חֶלְדַּי *enduring*.
1. The 12th captain for the monthly service in the sanctuary. He was descended from Othniel and is called "the Netophathite." B.C. 1015.
1 Ch. 27. 15 The..(captain) for the twelfth month..H.
2. An Israelite who returned from captivity and to whom special honour was given. In verse 14 his name appears to be changed to *Helem*. B.C. 519.
Zech. 6. 10 Take of (them of) the captivity..of H.

HE'-LEB, חֵלֶב *fat, or* חֵלֶב.
One of David's valiant men, from Netophah, S.E. of Jerusalem. B.C. 1048.
2 Sa. 23. 29 H. the son of Baanah, a Netophathite
1 Ch. 11. 30 H. the son of Baanah the Netophathite

HE'-LED, חֵלֶד. *The same as Heleb*.
1 Ch. 11. 30 H. the son of Baanah a Netophathite

HE'-LEK, חֵלֶק *portion*.
Second son of Gilead, and founder of the family of the Helekites, descended from Manasseh, Joseph's son. B.C. 1560.
Num. 26. 30 of H., the family of the Helekites
Josh. 17. 2 for the children of H., and for the children

HELL —
1. *The unseen state*, שְׁאוֹל *sheol*.
Deut 32. 22 and shall burn unto the lowest hell, and
2 Sa. 22. 6 The sorrows of hell compassed me about
Job 11. 8 what canst thou do? deeper than hell
26. 6 Hell (is) naked before him, and destruction
Psa. 9. 17 The wicked shall be turned into hell, (and)
16. 10 For thou wilt not leave my soul in hell
18. 5 The sorrows of hell compassed me about
55. 15 (and) let them go down quick into hell: for
86. 13 delivered my soul from the lowest hell
116. 3 and the pains of hell gat hold upon me
139. 8 If I make my bed in hell, behold, thou
Prov. 5. 5 down to death; her steps take hold on h.
7. 27 Her house (is) the way to hell, going down
9. 18 knoweth..her guests (are) in the depths of
15. 11 Hell and destruction (are) before the LORD
15. 24 that he may depart from hell beneath
23. 14 beat..and shalt deliver his soul from hell
27. 20 Hell and destruction are never full; so
Isa. 5. 14 Therefore hell hath enlarged herself, and
14. 9 Hell from beneath is moved for thee to
14. 15 Yet thou shalt be brought down to hell, to
28. 15 and with hell are we at agreement; when
28. 18 your agreement with hell shall not stand
57. 9 and didst debase (thyself even) unto hell
Eze. 31. 16 when I cast him down to hell with them
31. 17 They also went down into hell with him
32. 21 shall speak to him out of the midst of hell
32. 27 which are gone down to hell with their
Amos 9. 2 Though they dig into hell, thence shall
Jon. 2. 2 out of the belly of hell cried I, (and) thou
Hab. 2. 5 who enlargeth his desire as hell, and (is) as

2. *Hades, the unseen world*, ᾅδης *hades*.
Matt 11. 23 thou..shalt be brought down to hell: for
16. 18 gates of hell shall not prevail against it
Luke 10. 15 And thou..shalt be thrust down to hell
16. 23 in hell he lifted up his eyes, being in tor.
Acts 2. 27 thou wilt not leave my soul in hell, neither
2. 31 that his soul was not left in hell, neither
Rev. 1. 18 I..have the keys of hell and of death
6. 8 I looked..and Hell followed with him
20. 13 death and hell delivered up the dead
20. 14 death and hell were cast into the lake

3. *Valley of Hinnom, Gehinna*, γέεννα *geenna*.
Matt. 5. 22 shall say..shall be in danger of hell fire
5. 29, 30 thy whole body should be cast into h.
10. 28 him which is able to destroy..body in hell
18. 9 having two eyes to be cast into hell fire
23. 15 twofold more the child of hell than your.
23. 33 how can ye escape the damnation of hell?

This is part of the "hell" page (page 474) from my *Young's Analytical Concordance*. Note the two different Greek words (*hades* and *geenna*) both translated "hell." *Sheol*, on top, is the Hebrew equivalent of *hades*. The Greek word *Tartarus* appears on page 475. Whenever someone tells me to go to hell, I always ask them:

Which one?

as well as its Hebrew counterpart, *sheol*. There are no flames on the premises. Put your hand inside your pocket. Where is your hand? It's in hades. The words hell, heel, hole, hull, helmet, cell, cellar, holster, and hold (as of a ship), are all derived from the same root, *helan*. Examine these words individually and see how the idea of being covered, concealed or hidden, fits them all.

So where is the Capernaum that Jesus consigned to hades? There's nothing left of it. It ain't there. You can't see it. And that's the truth.

INVISIBLE

TRY THIS, FOR THE HELL OF IT

Let's say that an orthodox minister tells you that your father, who died three months ago, is in hell. This is a terrible lack of information. If you are a careful student of scripture, you will know that the King James, along with other versions, translated three different Greek words with the single English word "hell." As fond as you are of your father, you will want to know exactly where he is. No, this loosey-goosey hell talk will never do, especially as the orthodox minister intimates that your father will be there forever.

At this time, naturally, you will want to show the orthodox minister my Wonderfully Clear & Simple Chart on the following page. In your most respectful tone, you will want to ask the minister, "Pardon me, but which 'hell' is my father in? As you can see on this Wonderfully Clear & Simple Chart, the version you are using to locate my father has indiscriminately used this one English word to describe three different places. So, please, is my father in Tartarus, Gehenna, or the unseen?"

At this time, the orthodox minister will become very uncomfortable. The first thing he will try to do is change the subject, asking you where you got the book that contains the Wonderfully Clear & Simple Chart. You, then, will say, "Suppose I found it under my pillow? I do not see what difference it makes. Now, will you please answer my question?" You should not think it rude to answer in this way. It is the minister who was rude by telling you that your father was in hell without knowing what (the hell) he was talking about.

If the minister is lucky, he will remember somewhere he has to be. If he is unlucky, he will not remember. If he does not remember, you must now

Wonderfully Clear & Simple Chart
or
"Look Who's Stuck in Hell"

Passage	Greek Word	KJV	NIV	CLNT*
2 Peter 2:4	Tartaroo	hell	hell	Tartarus
Matthew 5:22	Geenna	hell	hell	Gehenna
Luke 16:23	hades	hell	hell	unseen

*Concordant Literal New Testament, my version of choice

stare at the minister. You must stare at him respectfully, yes, but stare nonetheless. This is hard to do, I realize, but the skill can be learned and perfected in front of a mirror at home. Neither should you say anything to the minister at this time. This is extremely hard to do. It will require great restraint not to babble something—anything—to make the orthodox minister feel better about struggling with his dark profession. But please do as I say. Stare at the minister and babble not. You will be doing him a favor, in the end.

If the minister says that your father is in Gehenna, you must say, as graciously as you can and with utter earnestness, "Then let us take a plane to Jerusalem and look for him there." If the minister says that your father is in Tartarus, remark that, while your father did, on occasion, fail to remember your mother's birthday, he was never a stubborn, sinning angel who surrendered his sovereignty during the days of Noah. (Counter the clergyman's stupefied expression by referring him to 1 Peter 3:19-20, 2 Peter, 2:4, and Jude 6). If the minister says that your father is in hades, let a smile come to your face and rejoice aloud in front of the startled cleric what good company your father is in. For he, like Christ (Acts 2:31), David (Psalm 16:10), and Jacob (Genesis 37:35) before him, has ceased from his troubles and sufferings (Job 3:11-19), and now rests, as if asleep (John 11:11, 14).

The parable of the Rich Man and Lazarus

For those unfamiliar with the passage, read Luke, chapter 16. Better yet, start at chapter 15. (I'll tell you why in a moment.) Jesus is telling a parable to sinners and Pharisees about a certain Rich Man who, in his lifetime, looked down on a poor, diseased man named Lazarus languishing at his gate. (The man was so bad off that dogs licked his sores. At least the dogs felt sorry for him.) Both men die. After death, Lazarus finds himself in Abraham's bosom, while the Rich Man writhes in a torment of flame. According to Christians, Jesus is telling a story here about two actual people. One of the people (Lazarus) is actually sitting on Abraham's chest, and the other (the Rich Man) is actually getting hot in a nearby fire, especially his tongue (verse 24). One would not expect a man roasting on an open fire to speak clearly or with forethought, yet the Rich Man does just that to Lazarus and Abraham. He has lots of questions, you see. Even while his flesh splits and crackles in the inferno, there are certain things this individual wishes to know. He has thoughts, questions, statements, puzzlements, and he is content to wait patiently for answers, swatting only occasionally at the nuisance fire. Lazarus is in no mood to talk, so it is Abraham who answers him, which is another remarkable feat, seeing that Abraham is an elderly man bearing another man of no mean age upon his chest.

"This is not a parable!" the Christians shout. "It is actually happening!" Well, no. It *is* a parable, and it is called that in Luke 15:3. Beginning in Luke,

chapter 15, Jesus embarks upon a fivefold parable designed to show Pharisees how badly they treated sinners.

The first part of the larger parable is the story of the ninety-nine sheep left in the fold by the shepherd, who seeks the one lost sheep. The Pharisees were supposed to think: *Gee. Maybe we're supposed to help sinners instead of condemning them.* The next installment of the fivefold parable is the woman with the ten coins who loses one. Big deal? To her it is. She wields a broom in her quest for the one lost coin. When she finds it, she calls her friends like it's kingdom come. The lesson to the Pharisees: *Heaven exults when one sinner repents; why don't you?* The next installment is the famous Prodigal Son story. It's a lot like the first two installments: *Sinner gets lost, God loves sinner, God restores sinner, everyone is happy except the Prodigal Son's brother and the Pharisees listening to the parable.* In the next two installments, Jesus shoots His sharpest arrows straight into the pharisaic liver. The parable of the Unjust Administrator (part four) informs the highbrows: *You are serving your own greed rather than the people of Israel.* The fifth installment (The Rich Man and Lazarus) is the cruelest cut of all: *You finely-dressed hypocrites will be cast from the kingdom, and the kingdom will be given to those producing fruit worthy of repentance, even if they are scumbags.*

Even before part five, most listeners knew what this was: an extended series of parables. Even the dumbest among them, by the time the Rich Man and Lazarus story rolled around, smacked their foreheads and said, *Oh, God. I see. Sorry. All this is a parable.* They knew dead people couldn't talk, especially not those with flaming tongues. Concerning the death state, the Jews' own scriptures testified: "There is no activity or planning or wisdom in the grave, where you are going" (Ecclesiastes 9:10).

From what I've said so far, you have to marvel at how anyone could take this parable literally. I take that back. I can see how it could happen. It could happen for the person who deep-down wants this to be a picture of the damned. God has set the trap. You'll remember I spoke earlier of how finely balanced God's revelation is. I said that if you want to see a particular thing, you will. All you have to do is blink or squint. Just one little oversight and— bang—you're deceived. What does God do to prevent this? Nothing. Again, He wants it to happen. He sends deceptions (2 Thessalonians 2:11-12) that all may be judged who do not believe the truth, but delight in injustice.

Allow me a small sidetrack here. I have often thought that if Jesus had just explained himself after saying, "This is My body," it would have saved the Catholics a lot of grief and wafer bills. For this is the religion that insists—with straight faces—that the factory-built wafer held aloft by the priest becomes—at the priest's bidding—the actual flesh of Jesus. What assertion could be more ridiculous? The world rolls its eyes. The Catholics, however, take their prized deception to magnificent lengths. If Jesus had only told the disciples, "Don't take this literally, lads. It's a common metaphor. Kind of like Isaiah writing, 'All flesh is grass.' Is all flesh literally grass? No. All flesh is *like* grass, because it withers away. It's a metaphor, and so is this. This bread I'm holding here is *like* My body, because it will be broken for you." Jesus could have held up the bread and said, "This is *like* My body," which would have been

a simile, and easier to grasp. But instead He said, "This *is* My body," employing the harder-to-see metaphor. Does He explain Himself? No. Either Jesus trusts that normal people will recognize a metaphor when they see one (and thus does not foresee the Catholic deception), or He wants the deception to arise, not for the sake of the deception, but that all may be judged who love ceremony and tradition over truth. I think He wanted the deception. And since the deception exists, it appears as though I'm right. ("All is of God"—2 Corinthians 5:18.)

As go the Catholics with the magical wafer, so go the Christians with the Rich Man and Lazarus. All Jesus had to do was use the word "parable" in front of Luke, chapter 16 (at the beginning of the Rich Man and Lazarus account), and not even the weeping ninnies at TBN would have gotten the wrong idea. Instead, He inspires Luke to put the word in front of what would become chapter 15 (there were no chapter headings in the original texts; all chapter headings are man-made), where this series of five parables begins, and then not use it again. Thus, by the time the fifth parable rolls around, those who want the Rich Man and Lazarus to be a picture of life after death have conveniently forgotten the opening paragraph (thanks, in part, to the obscuring factor of the artificial chapter heading, chapter

16). That opening paragraph is there, of course, for those who want to see it, but it's not there for those who like the idea of eternal torment. Magnificent! To me, this illustrates the genius of God.

So do not marvel at how Christians could take this parable literally. Marvel, instead, at the Christians' lack of consistency.

Go back to the goat nations of Matthew, chapter 25. Remember? They were banished to the outer reaches of the kingdom because they failed to help Israelites. When an Israelite was naked, these goats did not clothe them. When one was hungry or thirsty, not one goat ever gave them a sandwich or an iced tea. When an Israelite went to jail, all goat nations had something else to do. The sheep nations, on the other hand, did all the right things. And this is why they are blessed. *This is why they are blessed.* As I said before, there is no other criteria for blessing in the context other than, *Did you help Israel in her hour of need?*

Now, if Christians really believe that this is the Final Judgment, the Day of Decision, the Hour That Either Makes Or Breaks One's Eternal Destiny, I would think that hungry, naked, and incarcerated Jews would be having a field day. If bestowing physical blessings upon the sons of Abraham graduates one to sheephood and ensures one's "eternal life,"

SONS OF JACOB
(Sung to the tune of "Oh, Susannah!")

Oh I earn my own salvation
With a spigot and a cup.
If your name is Berg or Weissman
Then I'll fill your bladder up.

Sons of Jacob!
Your thirst is good for me.
For I come from a Christian background
Where we earn eternity.

then why not bless all the Semites one can? Why take the chance of missing one? Church newsletters ought to proclaim: "Take an Israelite to dinner—*your eternal life depends on it.*" Why not a "Feed the Jews" fest? I like this idea: "Visit Jacob in Jail—*or else!*" Or how about: "JOIN US SATURDAY FOR PASTOR DAVE'S '*HYDRATE AN ISRAELITE!*' PROGRAM. EARN YOUR ETERNAL SALVATION WITH A CANTEEN AND A STACK OF STYROFOAM CUPS!"

Back to the Rich Man and Lazarus. The Christian religion insists: "This is a picture of what happens to Christ-Acceptors and Christ-Rejecters after they die." If that's what they think, then *I* must insist they play by the rules and carefully study the criteria for becoming a Lazarus and avoiding the Rich Man's fate. Is the criteria, "Have faith in the cross of

"How you figure we're saved? Sure, we're poor an' hungry. But we ain't got no sores."

Jesus Christ?" No. How can it be, when the cross has yet to happen? There is nothing here at all about personal faith. There is nothing about believing in Jesus. Rather, Lazarus is "saved" and the Rich Man "damned" because 1) Lazarus was poor while the Rich Man was rich, 2) Lazarus wore ratty clothes while the Rich Man wore purple, 3) Lazarus was full of sores while the Rich Man lived comfortably, 4) Lazarus went hungry while the Rich Man had food, and 5) Lazarus got evil things in his life while the Rich Man got good.

If I were an earnest Christian locked into the orthodox deception, my sincere advice to those wishing to sit on Abraham's bosom for eternity would be: *Wear ratty clothes, obtain sores, get a dog to medicate you with its tongue, give up food, and make sure nothing good ever happens to you.*

"Then will I be saved, Master Martin?"

"Yes, my son. Verily, verily. Then you will be saved."

"**And whosoever was not found written in the book of life was cast into the lake of fire**" (Revelation 20:15).

I shift now from the words of Jesus and turn briefly to the apostle John. Jesus spoke many more threats, judgments, and exhortations. I have not listed them all because I'm teaching you to fish. I'm trying to do the same with the "eternals" and "forevers" scattered throughout scripture. Allow me another brief sidetrack here.

There are many more "eternals" and "forevers" in scripture, but now that you have the key, you can go it alone. "Eonian" is the proper translation across the board, even in "difficult" places like Romans 16:26, when God is called "the eonian God." Stop and think it through. The proper translation of Romans 16:26 ("the eonian God") doesn't make God *un*eternal. He's just not called eternal *here*. This verse is telling us something different, that He's the God of time. I think that's comforting. He's not only the God of eternity, He's the God of now. The comfort comes when we let the verse speak. By forcing it to sing, that is, to work outside its natural parameter, we miss its blessing. God is the God of time as well as eternity. If you want eternity, go to Psalm 102:27, "His years have no end." Don't try to make Romans 16:26 do what Psalm 102:27 has already done.

Use this key on all the doors; the locks are the same. To return to the fishing analogy, bait your hook and cast at will. Once you know how to do it, you can eat anytime you want. Once you realize Jesus preached upon a time issue rather than eternity, all scripture will make new sense to you. Brilliant new vistas will open.

Jesus' earthly ministry, amazingly, will bless you the more when you properly limit it. Don't feel bad about it. Jesus Himself wants you to do it. *WWJD?* He would exhort you to accept His own testimony concerning His earthly purpose. Go ahead and do it. You won't hurt His feelings. You will be doing both Him and yourself a favor. How? It will cause the later revelations given to Paul to make sense to you. You'll no longer have to ignore Paul in order to believe Jesus. The clash between law and grace will disappear, as well. Yes. This is the key to that. Law here, grace there; don't mix them. God's means will no longer be taken for His goals when you realize the time element of Jesus' ministry. Imagine how wonderful it will be believing all of scripture, rather than sweeping half of it under your particular religion's rug. Well, you're there. Thank God.

The lake of fire scares people, and I guess it should. Admittedly, it's not a happy place. If only we knew what it was. Well, we do. So many people say, "Oh, God's judgments are such a mystery." Then they say, "We just can't figure out God." I agree that we can't understand whatever God refuses to tell us, but what He does tell us is readily known. He, Himself, defines the lake of fire in Revelation 20:14—

"This is the second death—the lake of fire." Rarely is God so obvious. This is not a mystery. My eleven year-old understands it, and so does his five year-old cousin. The lake of fire is the second death. What is the second death? It's the same as the first death, just more of it. What is the first death? Go to a funeral home and stare at the corpse; that's the first death.

Those to whom God does not give faith in this lifetime, rise to be judged at the great white throne. (God is still their Savior—1 Timothy 4:10.) This occurs after the thousand-years are finished. Remember Revelation 20:5? "The rest of the dead do not live until the thousand years should be finished." They are resurrected and judged at the great white throne. (God is still their Savior—1 Timothy 4:10.) Those whose names are not written in the book of life are cast into the lake of fire. This sounds like a scene from a Stephen King movie, but it's not. (God is still their Savior—1 Timothy 4:10.) It's quick and painless—note "cast" versus "dragged." Jesus equated death with sleep, and that's what the second death is: unconsciousness. The dead do not feel pain. They are unaware of the passage of time. They do not worry about things. (God is still their Savior—1 Timothy 4:10.) They do not fret over loved ones. They are neither cold, hot, nor tired. They do not writhe, not even a little. And they definitely do not stay dead forever. Why? Because the second death is eventually abolished. That's not me talking, it's 1 Corinthians 15:26. And 1 Timothy 4:10 assures us that "God is the Savior of all mankind."

If these second-deathers—the last members of humanity to be given faith—are not eventually raised to immortality to live forever with God, then God is not the Savior of all mankind. But since He is (1 Timothy 4:10), then these people must eventually be delivered out of death. And they are, because "the last enemy is being abolished: death" (1 Corinthians 15:26). Honestly, my eleven year-old son hums happy tunes to this. It only seems complicated when trying to untangle the mixed-up contradictions people were raised on. Besides, God must become all in all (1 Corinthians 15:28). And He will.

Only three individuals are tormented alive in the lake of fire. Out comes the light again, and watch where it points: *Only three individuals are tormented alive in the lake of fire.* These three are clearly stated to be (in Revelation 20:10), "the Adversary (Satan), the wild beast, and the false prophet." If everyone is tormented there, why say there are three? Interesting that the lake of fire is not called the second death until verse fourteen, when humans are cast there. These beings of verse ten are not human. They are supernatural beings, the only beings able to stand such a trial alive.

Why do Christians say that everyone is tormented in the lake of fire, when scripture says there are only three? Speaking relatively again, it is because they are careless. It is because they cannot be bothered with minute detail. It is because they are too eager and apt to accept whatever their pastors tell them. It is because, frankly Scarlet, they don't give a damn. Uncle Harry needs punished for his sins, and if the lake of fire can somehow be adapted to the task, why fuss with facts? *Uncle Harry deserves it. Dumb cluck. He had his chance and blew it. I had my chance and delivered faith on demand.*

The problem (one of many) is that the Christians did not create Uncle Harry. They did not form Harry in the womb in the likeness of their own image. The Christians did not die for Uncle Harry; that's one of the problems here. They did not promise to bring him into the fold, even if he were the last sheep afield on Earth. And thus, the Christians will not aim with care this fiery lake. In fact, were it a Tommy gun, they would strafe with it. The compassion is so missing here that learning of Harry's eventual reconciliation will disappoint the followers of Christ. *I served Jesus all my life! And you're telling me that* Harry *is getting in? I'm sorry, but my accomplishment of getting to heaven has just been drastically cheapened.*

Great. When it reaches zero, you'll have learned the truth.

Scripture says that the Adversary, the wild beast, and the false prophet are to be "tormented day and night for the eons of the eons" (Revelation 20:10). Of course, the King James Version does not say that, and neither does the NIV or the NASB. These versions define the duration of torment as, "day and night, forever and ever." Here is the time-versus-eternity issue again, the God-sent penny that potentially wrecks the train. Let's shine light on the phrase "day and night," as it is the overlooked key. This is a time phrase. It works perfectly with "eons of the eons," which is also a time phrase, but fails with "forever and ever," which is anything but.

Speaking of failure, if "forever" means eternity, then what does "and ever" mean? Eternity and then some? Eternity with an eternity to spare? If a sentence is insane, be assured it's unscriptural. The phrase "eons of the eons" is the scriptural one; it's the one God wrote before pulling the veil. It's of the same grammatical construction as "king of kings" and "holies of holies." (See how God provides the out? The tool? He veils the critical "eons of the eons," yet leaves the identically constructed "holies of holies" intact. This construction is evident only in the Greek, for which you'll need another tool. But the tool always exists. There's always a key laying around, or a screwdriver. God does not pull a veil without providing an opposing cord.) A big plus in favor of this construction is that it makes sense. A king of kings is one great king among other kings. Holies of holies are great holy places among several lesser ones. Likewise, eons of the eons are two eons excelling other eons. The three evil entities mentioned earlier will be tormented for two eons (the first being the tail end of the eon that includes the thousand-year kingdom, the second being the eon of the new heavens and the new earth—see Revelation 21:1). The torment continues until these beings are no longer evil.

The explanation may not be that simple, but the principle behind it is: *Supervised trial results in change for the better.* We are not seeing senseless, continual punishment here, but remedial discipline at the hand of God.

Where does the love of God stop? (Answer out loud.) You're right, it doesn't. It keeps rolling until its objects are consumed and changed by it. Why should it be different with these premier sinners? Were you not once a premier sinner? And was it not some trial in your life that brought you to faith? Was it not some desperate need, a hard, pressing thing, that drove you to Christ? All right, then. Why deny these the same experience?

Am I suggesting that Satan himself shall be delivered from the lake of fire with a changed heart, to be granted an eternity of praising God at his Creator's throne? No. I am insisting upon it. God is not only the Savior of all mankind, but also the reconciler of all creation (Colossians 1:20, Romans 8:21). The means of this blessing is the cross of His Son, Jesus

Christ. This is why Christ suffered so much. This is why He was whipped and spat upon, nailed up naked before His mother, then forsaken by His God. It was for this kind of sin. If Satan is not reached and reconciled with so awful an effort, it would mean the failure of the cross. Are you prepared to admit to the failure of the cross? "*Hell is for sinners!*" people have told me. My God, what ignorance. The *cross* is for sinners.

And it worked.

Do you think *you* will be praising God loudly and on high? You have not heard anything. Wait until you hear the voice of one bound for eons as His ultimate enemy. *He who has been forgiven much, loves much.* But so it is with God and enemies. He heeds His own principles. By this I mean to say, He loves His enemies.

Jesus did not "tell all" while on earth. According to His own confession, He limited Himself— during His brief years in flesh—to Israel and the proclamation of the thousand-year kingdom. Does this mean He had nothing more to say? No. From His exalted position at the right hand of God, Christ apprehended a sinner named Saul—a man on his

way to Damascus to murder saints—and over-
whelmed him with a grace unfathomed. He dusted
him off, changed his name to Paul, and whispered
into his ear a secret, a message beyond the thousand-year kingdom, beyond the red-lettered threats
of the Palestine Jesus, beyond the sacrifices of Israel,
beyond the rejection of disobedient Jews, beyond
Gehenna and the second death, beyond anything
that had ever touched the thread of human hearing.
Let us hear the amazing testimony from Paul himself:

> Yes, to me, less than the least of all the saints,
> has God given this grace, to enable me to proclaim to
> the nations the gospel of the incalculable riches of Christ,
> and to make plain to all men the meaning of that divine
> secret which He Who created everything has kept hid-
> den from the creation until now...For God has allowed
> us to know the secret of His plan, and it is this: He pur-
> posed long ago in His sovereign will that all human his-
> tory should be consummated in Christ, that everything
> that exists in Heaven or earth should find its perfection
> and fulfillment in Him (Ephesians 3:8-9, 1:9-10).

What revelation could be higher? I doubt that
you have ever seen these words, and I think I know
why. It is because such sayings of engulfing grace
clash so impossibly with the law of limited blessing

set forth by the dusty Nazarene carpenter, that your
pastor couldn't reconcile them. Instead of emphasiz-
ing the grace ("can't trust people with too much of
it"), your teacher swept such verses under the church
welcome mat and focused on the law. But the Man
of Nazareth is not all Christ is. It is part, but not all.
You must see revelation as progressive. Keep reading.
The law was only a tutor to lead us to Christ. God is
always doing new things. He wants you to follow.
His full-orbed revelation, the secret of His innermost
will, was held like wine, corked until its time. Jesus
Himself said to Nicodemus, "If I told you of the
terrestrial and you are not believing, how shall you
be believing if I should be telling you of the celestial?" He did not tell him. Israel could not even grasp
her own calling, let alone this. But the time did come.
On a Monday, or a Tuesday, or perhaps on a Wednes-
day morning before dawn, a young radical named
Saul packed for Damascus.

I am not pitting Christ's words against those of
Paul. The words of Paul *are* the words of Christ, yet
they are higher words, purposely better, words that
intentionally reach outward and away, beyond the
pale of Israel, Time, and Earth:

> *As in Adam all are dying, thus also in Christ shall
> all be vivified, yet every man in his own order* —1

Corinthians 15:22-23

Even as, through the disobedience of the one man, the many were constituted sinners, thus also, through the obedience of the One, the many shall be constituted just —Romans 5:19

For there is one God, and one Mediator of God and mankind, a Man, Christ Jesus, Who is giving Himself a correspondent Ransom for all, the testimony in its own eras —1 Timothy 2:5-6

God is the Savior of all mankind, especially of believers —1 Timothy 4:10

God locks up all together in stubbornness, that He should be merciful to all —Romans 11:32

All is out of God, through God, and into God — Romans 11:36

All in heaven and on earth shall be headed up in Christ —Ephesians 1:10

Everything created will be reconciled to God, through the blood of His cross —Colossians 1:16-20, Romans 8:21

In the name of Jesus every knee should be bowing, celestial and terrestrial and subterranean, and every tongue should be acclaiming that Jesus Christ is Lord, for the glory of God, the Father —Philippians 2:10-11

Glory.

I have dedicated my life to exposing religion and promoting the cross. I don't want applause, just an ear. And you have given me that. And for that, I thank you.

Many fine scholars have written on this topic. The return of all creation to God is an old truth (after all, Paul taught it), embraced by many over the centuries. Read the church fathers, and you will find it. It used to be the common belief, believe it or not. The doctrine of eternal torment crept in only after the Greek scriptures got translated into Latin. This was, as you know, an act of God. It had to happen, to expose hearts.

I am just another herald of the cross. I do not often think of myself as a scholar, though I might be. I am first and foremost a writer, a communicator. Most scholars I know speak in the complicated language of DOS. I am Windows, with all the happy little icons. If I have put too light a face on this weighty theme, I apologize. But when God put His finger on me twenty years ago, He said, "You will be the clown outside the tent." That was God's original metaphor for me; a clown. I thought at the time, *Okay, God. That's fine. I do like the crazy shoes. If I can at least introduce people to Your glories, I'll be happy.* There are many scholarly works you can turn to, and I encourage you to do so. I include a couple of resources at the end, when I finish my own Barnum & Bailey testimony.

For many, it is a shock to see the common beliefs exposed, and to realize how many are deceived. Even more shocking is finding God Himself behind the deception. Does this make God a deceiver? It does not. His essence is love. Scripture says God kills (1 Samuel 2:6); does that make Him a killer? It would be unfair to call Him that. It's not His essence. Read the rest of 1 Samuel 2:6—He kills only to make alive. The killing is a necessary prelude to resurrection. We should look beyond God's means and toward His goals, for these always justify His hardest paths. Thus also with deception. It is the precursor of revelation. Deception is the litmus with which God tests hearts. Do we really love truth, or do we love our religions and social comforts? God, in His mercy, will expose us to ourselves. This may be painful, but it is for our own good, and for the glory of God.

The shock is finding Christianity in wholesale apostasy. Yet this is in accord with scriptural precedent. The religious majority is always wrong, always. Not sometime, but every time. Study the biblical precedent. Nothing has changed.

In 1 Timothy 4:1-2, Paul prophesied of a time of "withdrawing from the faith," when those naming Christ will "give heed to deceiving spirits and the teachings of demons, in the hypocrisy of false expressions." It would be an era "when they will not tolerate sound teaching, but, their hearing being tickled, they will heap up for themselves teachers in accord with their own desires, and, indeed, they will be turning their hearing away from the truth, yet will be turned aside to myths" (2 Timothy 4:3-4). Christians everywhere stand guard against this, determined to prevent it. They stare at their watches, waiting for it to arrive. The sad truth is that it arrived shortly after Paul's death, and is flourishing today in their midst.

The world hates God, not because God is hateable, but because of the picture Christianity has painted of Him. The doctrine of eternal torment is a teaching of demons; a myth. It infects the world via a series of false expressions, printed onto tracts and forced into sermons. Those who espouse and teach it are in full heed of deceiving spirits, though they know it not. There must be a remedy, and there is. 2 Timothy 2:15, **"Be diligent to present yourself approved to God as a workman who does not need to be ashamed, handling accurately the word**

of truth."

He who has an ear, let him hear what the Spirit is saying.

The Concordant Literal New Testament is my version of choice. It's the most accurate translation in the world. Operating on the principle that God 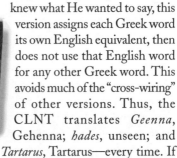 knew what He wanted to say, this version assigns each Greek word its own English equivalent, then does not use that English word for any other Greek word. This avoids much of the "cross-wiring" of other versions. Thus, the CLNT translates *Geenna*, Gehenna; *hades*, unseen; and *Tartarus*, Tartarus—every time. If one is willing to look up every word in a concordance to see whether the original word was uniformly translated, the KJV and other versions do work. Better, however, is to read and study with a version that translates uniformly to begin with. In addition, the CLNT contains its own 330 page concordance in the back, so that students can check the translation method for themselves.

The Concordant Literal New Testament is available with an accompanying Concordant Greek Text. The CGT contains an actual reproduction of the best available Greek text. You can see the Greek letters and words right on the page. But you don't need to read Greek, because there is word-for-word English running beneath the original. The English words are brought directly down, in the order of the original Greek. This makes the CGT ultra-literal. It's great for study, but generally unsuitable for casual reading. Here's a portion of John 3:16:

The CLNT is based upon this literal-literal rendering. Where words have been added in the CLNT to make this readable, lightface type is used. This way, students can see which words are in the original text, and which words have been added. Once again, this is not a thing you want to read devotionally, but it's pretty cool to be looking at the actual Greek. Just carrying this volume makes you dangerous at Bible studies.

These tools, as well as other study aids and literature, may be had from the Concordant Publishing Concern. Their street address is 15570 Knochaven Road, Santa Clarita, CA, 91350. The web site is: www.concordant.org.

Another worthy site with lots of informative articles: www.godstruthfortoday.org.

Happy seeking.

P.S. See the piece of paper taped onto the front of my Bible on the previous page? I've had that there for years. It's a quote from Francis Bacon that especially applies to this discussion of eternal torment. I think it fitting to close with it:

> "Whosoever shall entertain
> high and vaporous imaginations
> instead of a laborious and sober
> inquiry of truth, shall beget
> hopes and beliefs of
> strange and impossible shapes."

--Francis Bacon

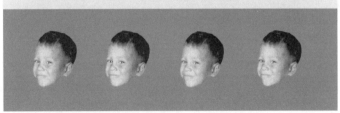

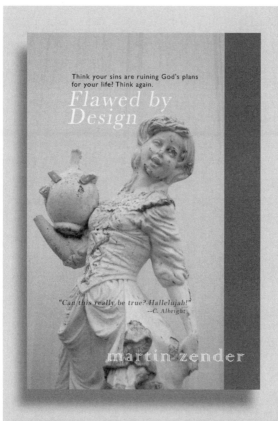

Think your sins are ruining God's plans
for your life? Think again.

Flawed by
Design

"Can this really be true? Hallelujah!"
—C. Albright

martin zender